Contents

Any words appearing in the text in bold, like this, are explained in the Glossary.

Pollution issues around the world

NORTH
AMERICA

Read page 31 to find out how the dumping of **toxic** chemicals created a major **environmental** hazard at Love Canal in the United States.

Learn on page 25 how pollution has caused a giant dead zone in the waters of part of the Gulf of Mexico.

ATLANTIC
OCEAN

Pollution prevents millions of people having access to clean, safe water supplies. Read on page 8 about how polluted water helped spread the disease of **cholera** throughout Peru in the early 1990s.

SOUTH
AMERICA

PACIFIC
OCEAN

N

MOWBRAY GARDENS MOW

ESSURE

ON

www.raintreepublishers.co.uk

Visit our website to find out more information about **Raintree** books.

To order:

☎ Phone 44 (0) 1865 888113

📄 Send a fax to 44 (0) 1865 314091

💻 Visit the Raintree bookshop at **www.raintreepublishers.co.uk** to browse our catalogue and order online.

First published in Great Britain by Raintree, Halley Court, Jordan Hill, Oxford OX2 8EJ, part of Harcourt Education.
Raintree is a registered trademark of Harcourt Education Ltd.

© Harcourt Education Ltd 2006
First published in paperback in 2007
The moral right of the proprietor has been asserted.

Editorial: Sarah Shannon
and Louise Galpine
Design: Lucy Owen and Bridge
Creative Services Ltd
Picture Research: Natalie Gray
and Sally Cole
Production: Chloe Bloom

Originated by Repro Multi Warna
Printed and bound in China by South China Printing Company

ISBN 1 844 43974 7 (hardback)
10 09 08 07 06
10 9 8 7 6 5 4 3 2 1

ISBN 1 844 439 81 X (paperback)
ISBN 978 1 844 43981 2 (paperback)
11 10 09 08 07
11 10 9 8 7 6 5 4 3 2 1

British Library Cataloguing in Publication Data
Gifford, Clive
Pollution. - (Planet Under Pressure)
363.7'3

A full catalogue record for this book is available from the British Library.

Acknowledgements
The publishers would like to thank the following for permission to reproduce photographs: Alamy pp. **10–11** (Bryan & Cherry Alexander); Corbis pp. **14–15;** Corbis pp. **20–21** (W. Geiersperger), **24–25** (Nathan Benn), **28–29** (Angelo Harnak), **30–31** (Ashley Cooper), **36–37** (Keren Su), **12-13** (Steve Marcus/Las Vegas Sun/Reuters); Corbis/Bettmann pp. **16–17;** Corbis/Sygma pp. **38–39** (Les Stone); DEBKUSHAL/UNEP/Still Pictures pp. **3–4, 6–7;** Digital Vision/Harcourt Education pp. **24–25;** Empics/EPA pp. **16–17, 36–37;** Environmental Images pp. **36** (Herbert Girardet); Panos pp. **8–9** (Mark Henley), **26-27** (Caroline Penn), **32-33** (Karen Robinson); Panos/Visum pp. **22–23** (Ludwig Gerd); Science Photo Library pp. **28–29** (Simon Fraser); Science Photo Library/NOAA pp. **18–19;** Still Pictures pp. **10–11** (Al Grillo), **40, 42, 44, 46** (Mark Edwards), **34–35** (Hartmut Schwarzbach), **40–41** (Ray Pfortner).

Cover photograph of pipe with pollution reproduced with kind permission of Getty and of city with heavy pollution from pipes with kind permission of Still Pictures.

Every effort has been made to contact copyright holders of any material reproduced in this book. Any omissions will be rectified in subsequent printings if notice is given to the publishers.

Disclaimer
All the Internet addresses (URLs) given in this book were valid at the time of going to press. However, due to the dynamic nature of the Internet, some addresses may have changed, or sites may have changed or ceased to exist since publication. While the author and publishers regret any inconvenience this may cause readers, no responsibility for any such changes can be accepted by either the author or the publishers.

Dedicated to the memory of Lucy Owen

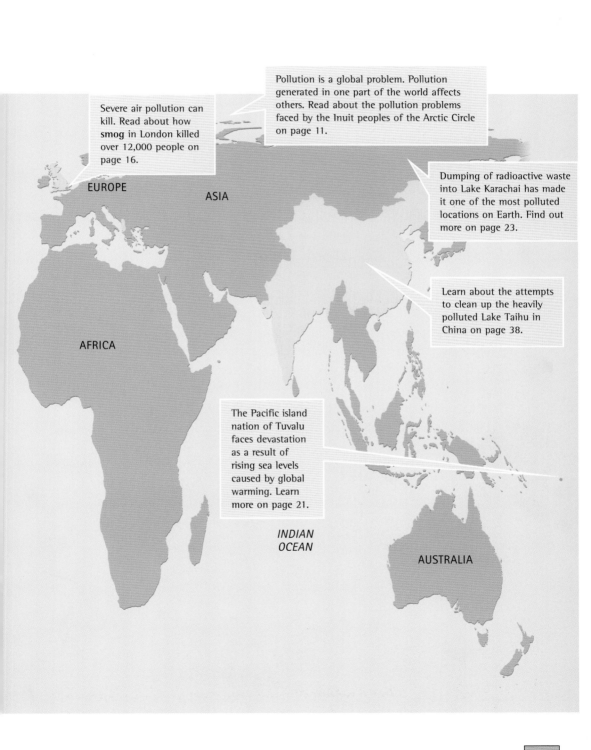

Severe air pollution can kill. Read about how **smog** in London killed over 12,000 people on page 16.

Pollution is a global problem. Pollution generated in one part of the world affects others. Read about the pollution problems faced by the Inuit peoples of the Arctic Circle on page 11.

Dumping of radioactive waste into Lake Karachai has made it one of the most polluted locations on Earth. Find out more on page 23.

Learn about the attempts to clean up the heavily polluted Lake Taihu in China on page 38.

The Pacific island nation of Tuvalu faces devastation as a result of rising sea levels caused by global warming. Learn more on page 21.

EUROPE

ASIA

AFRICA

INDIAN OCEAN

AUSTRALIA

A global problem

Pollution occurs all over the planet on land, in water, and at both low and high **altitudes** in the Earth's **atmosphere**. Pollution is the introduction of a substance or energy at levels that cause harm to living things or the **environment**. Scientists think of pollution mainly in terms of the introduction of pollutants by human activity. Pollution can vary in scale from a single car's exhaust **emissions**, to a giant factory pumping thousands of litres of chemical waste water into rivers.

Wrong place, wrong amount

A "pollutant" may occur harmlessly in nature but when it is released into a certain location, or at too high a concentration, it has harmful effects. For instance, ozone performs a useful role high in the atmosphere, but if it is released at ground level, ozone can be a dangerous pollutant.

Sometimes, the amount, concentration, or location of a substance is what gives rise to pollution. For example, carbon dioxide (CO_2) occurs in nature and is part of the collection of gases which make up our atmosphere. People, animals, and plants generate it naturally as a by-product of **respiration**. However, over the last 200 years, the burning of **fossil fuels** has sent millions of tonnes of extra carbon dioxide into the atmosphere. This additional carbon dioxide has resulted in the **enhanced greenhouse effect**, which is a major part of **global warming** (see page 20).

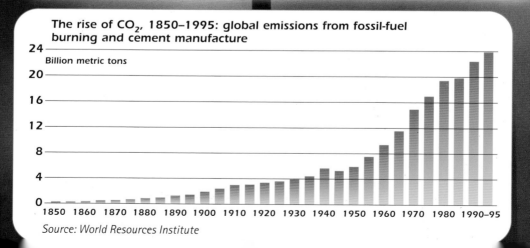

The rise of CO_2, 1850–1995: global emissions from fossil-fuel burning and cement manufacture

Billion metric tons

24 — 20 — 16 — 12 — 8 — 4 — 0

1850 1860 1870 1880 1890 1900 1910 1920 1930 1940 1950 1960 1970 1980 1990–95

Source: World Resources Institute

Carrying chemicals

Chemicals enter people's bodies from the air they breathe, the water they drink, and the food they eat. A cocktail of potentially harmful man-made chemicals was found in the blood of all 155 volunteers tested in a 2003 UK study. The highest number of chemicals found in any one person was 49 and the average number was about 30. Many of these chemicals are not easily broken down and remain in people's bodies. For example, 99 per cent of the people tested had chemical products in their blood from the **pesticide** DDT which was banned in the UK in 1986.

Source: New Scientist, 2003

When did pollution start?

Pollution is not new. Ever since humans started consuming the planet's **resources**, there has been some pollution. In the past, the impact on the planet was minimal. Smoke from fires, human **sewage** in water, and other pollutants were gradually broken down or absorbed by the environment. But as the world population grew and started to settle together in large towns and cities, local pollution became a problem.

COAL

One of the earliest recorded instances of **urban** air pollution was in the 12th century. People in London began to burn coal instead of wood. It caused enough choking smoke and smog for the King of England, Edward I, to threaten coal burners with execution. Later, in 1880, London again suffered severe air pollution from coal burning, resulting in over 2,000 deaths.

WATER-BORNE PROBLEMS

Many of the world's early urban areas had little or no sewage treatment or waste disposal systems. Waste and sewage flowing into rivers polluted the water, making it undrinkable and providing ideal conditions for deadly diseases. **Cholera** thrives in sewage-polluted water: it is spread by **ingesting** water, food, or any other material containing bacteria from the human waste of a cholera victim. Polluted water caused a cholera epidemic which swept through South America in 1991 and killed 2,720 people in Peru, and a further 4,000 in neighbouring countries.

Top ten most polluted cities, 2000

1. Lanzhou, China
2. Guangzhou, China
3. Shanghai, China
4. Xian, China
5. Shenyang, China
6. Mumbai, India
7. Kolkata, India
8. Mexico City, Mexico
9. Seoul, South Korea
10. New Delhi, India

Source: World Health Organization

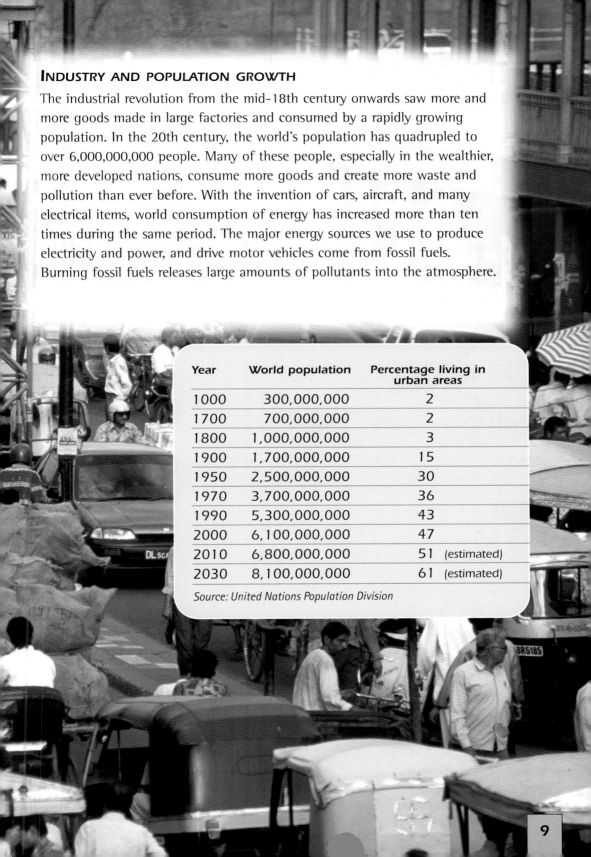

INDUSTRY AND POPULATION GROWTH

The industrial revolution from the mid-18th century onwards saw more and more goods made in large factories and consumed by a rapidly growing population. In the 20th century, the world's population has quadrupled to over 6,000,000,000 people. Many of these people, especially in the wealthier, more developed nations, consume more goods and create more waste and pollution than ever before. With the invention of cars, aircraft, and many electrical items, world consumption of energy has increased more than ten times during the same period. The major energy sources we use to produce electricity and power, and drive motor vehicles come from fossil fuels. Burning fossil fuels releases large amounts of pollutants into the atmosphere.

Year	World population	Percentage living in urban areas	
1000	300,000,000	2	
1700	700,000,000	2	
1800	1,000,000,000	3	
1900	1,700,000,000	15	
1950	2,500,000,000	30	
1970	3,700,000,000	36	
1990	5,300,000,000	43	
2000	6,100,000,000	47	
2010	6,800,000,000	51	(estimated)
2030	8,100,000,000	61	(estimated)

Source: United Nations Population Division

A global issue

For many years, pollution was thought of as a local problem. But a series of major environmental accidents began to change people's thinking. Major oil spills from tankers, such as the *Torrey Canyon* and *Exxon Valdez*, which devastated coastal wildlife and communities, were worldwide news. So were the fears of radiation pollution (see page 23) from accidents and leaks at nuclear power plants, or during the transportation of radioactive waste.

After an oil spill, oil clogs the feathers of birds and the fur of animals, destroying their warming properties. Many animals then die from the cold. Other creatures consume the oil trying to clean themselves, or eat food coated in oil which poisons them. Oil can also suffocate fish and other sea creatures.

As the 20th century progressed, scientists and environmentalists realised that pollution occurred on a global scale. Public awareness was raised by reports of how certain toxic chemicals, such as **insecticides**, were used in one area but transported via water or air over vast distances. Scientists discovered, for instance, that in remote parts of Greenland, 1,600 kilometres (994 miles) from the nearest major road, lead particles blown by car exhausts had been trapped in the ice in air bubbles.

During the late 1970s and the 1980s, three major global pollution issues emerged: the hole in the **ozone layer** (see page 18), **acid rain** (page 18), and global warming (page 20). All three of these environmental problems cross national boundaries and affect whole regions, continents, or even the entire planet.

Arctic Circle polluted by Asia, America, and Africa

Pollutants from as far away as Mexico and China are threatening the traditional food sources of the native Inuit peoples living inside the Arctic Circle. Harmful agricultural pesticides have been carried by wind across oceans and continents to the frozen Arctic, which scientists believe acts as a sponge for a wide range of pollutants. Some of these pollutants find their way into the **food chain** where they are carried in animal fats. The traditional Inuit diet is based heavily on animal fats from fish and sea mammals, such as seals. A report by the Canadian Polar Commission warns that concentrations of these substances could reach dangerous levels in the next few decades.

Pollution today

In recent times, most countries have passed laws or started initiatives to combat rising levels of pollution. As the following chapters show, there are many things people, governments, and industries can do to help prevent and reduce pollution. But the problem of pollution is still a growing one. It affects millions of people's health and the land or water they rely on to survive.

Air pollution

The **atmosphere** is the mixture of gases which surround a body in space. Other planets have an atmosphere but, so far, Earth is the only planet known to possess an atmosphere capable of supporting life. Its gases are essential for the functioning of almost all living things. The atmosphere also plays a key role in the water cycle (see page 22), whilst winds and air currents transport rain around the globe. The atmosphere also shields the planet's surface from certain harmful rays from the Sun, whilst trapping enough heat to warm the planet for life to flourish.

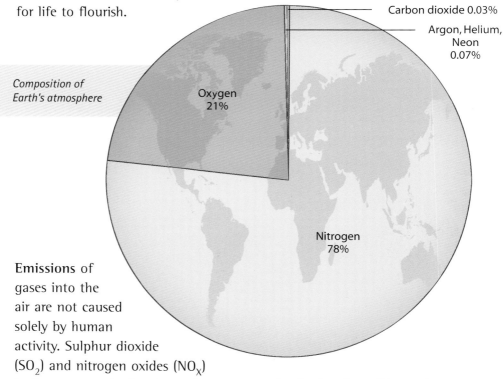

Composition of Earth's atmosphere

Carbon dioxide 0.03%

Argon, Helium, Neon 0.07%

Oxygen 21%

Nitrogen 78%

Emissions of gases into the air are not caused solely by human activity. Sulphur dioxide (SO_2) and nitrogen oxides (NO_x) both can occur in the atmosphere as a result of volcanic activity and the decay of dead animals and plants. The world's 1,300,000,000 cattle generate as much as 20 per cent of the total **methane** sent into the atmosphere. It is only in the past 250 years, since the world has **industrialized**, the world population boomed, and large areas of forest have been cleared, that air pollution emissions have risen to their current threatening levels.

The most polluted city in the United States

In 2004, a report by the American Lung Association ranked Los Angeles as the United States city with the worst air pollution. The city ranked worst in both smog levels and particle pollution (the microscopic particles produced by wood burning, diesel exhaust, power plant emissions, and various other sources). According to the report, more than 25 per cent of Americans live in areas with unhealthy particle pollution levels. Nearly 50 per cent live in areas where the smog levels are considered health-threatening. In 2005, a separate study found that people in the most polluted sections of Los Angeles were more likely to suffer from asthma, diabetes, and fatal heart disease. Researchers attribute the higher pollution levels to the city's size, number of vehicles, and location. Traffic congestion is common in the commuter-heavy city of 13 million people. Because the city sits in a valley surrounded by mountains, researchers believe this helps trap the pollution.

What are the main air pollutants?

There are many different air pollutants which cause harm at different locations in the atmosphere. Some of them are:

Carbon dioxide (CO_2) produced in nature, but also by the burning of **fossil fuels** and wood. Apart from being the major **greenhouse gas**, rare, low-level clouds of carbon dioxide can kill. In 1986 a carbon dioxide cloud caused by volcanic activity around Lake Nyos in Cameroon killed 1,800 people.

Carbon monoxide (CO) produced by the incomplete burning of wood and fossil fuels in transport. It lowers the amount of oxygen that enters blood and mainly affects the heart and nervous system. Large quantities can cause death.

Chlorofluorocarbons (CFCs) are gases that are released mainly from air-conditioning systems, aerosols, and refrigeration. When emitted into the higher atmosphere they react with other substances to damage the **ozone layer**. At a lower level, they add to the **enhanced greenhouse effect.**

Lead (Pb) is present in some fuels, lead batteries, paints, and many other products. It can cause damage to the nervous system and digestive problems, and, in some cases, cancer. It particularly affects children.

Nitrogen oxides (NO_x) help cause smog and acid rain. They are produced from burning fuels including petrol, diesel, and coal. Nitrogen oxides, particularly nitrogen dioxide (NO_2), can cause major breathing problems, such as severe asthma.

Ozone (O_3) occurs naturally in the upper layers of the atmosphere but ground-level ozone, produced by pollutants from vehicles and industries, is a dangerous part of smog causing eye irritation, breathing problems, and diseases.

Particulate matter (PM) consists of tiny solid particles in the air in the form of smoke, dust, and vapour that can remain suspended for long periods. PM10s are a type of particulate matter which can lodge in lungs, cause severe health problems, and even kill.

Sulphur dioxide (SO_2) is a gas produced mainly from burning coal in power plants and in industry. It is a major contributor to **smog** and **acid rain.** Sulphur dioxide can lead to lung diseases.

Major volcanic eruptions can send ash, soot, smoke, and chemicals high into the atmosphere. The 1991 eruption of Mount Pinatubo in the Philippines threw ash some 32 kilometres (20 miles) up into the atmosphere. Yet such natural emissions of gases are generally absorbed by the Earth's atmosphere.

What is smog?

Smog is a mixture of air pollutants which can build up to extremely harmful concentrations, especially in crowded, urban areas. Smog often produces a haze which is difficult to see through. It can contain pollutants such as ammonia, nitrogen dioxide, carbon monoxide, and sulphur dioxide. However, the two most common and lethal are ground-level ozone and particulate matter (PM). Ground-level ozone is formed from complicated reactions in the air just above the Earth's surface, involving nitrogen oxides and volatile organic compounds (VOCs).

Killer smog in Donora, USA

In 1948, waste from a number of industries (including a zinc production plant and a steel mill) created a thick, heavily polluted smog over the valley of Donora, in the American state of Pennsylvania. In five days over 6,000 illnesses were registered and 20 people died.

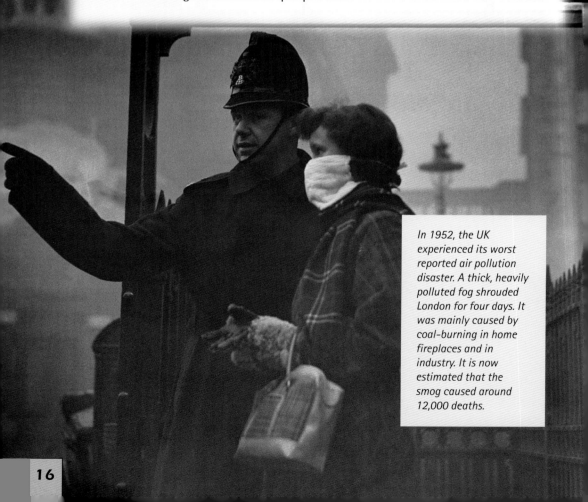

In 1952, the UK experienced its worst reported air pollution disaster. A thick, heavily polluted fog shrouded London for four days. It was mainly caused by coal-burning in home fireplaces and in industry. It is now estimated that the smog caused around 12,000 deaths.

WHY IS URBAN AIR POLLUTION SUCH A CONCERN?

Many of the key air pollutants that cause health problems are given off by motor vehicles and the burning of fossil fuels. When people and vehicles are crammed together in small areas, air pollution can rise to dangerous levels.

"Clean air" laws and cleaner fuels and cars initiatives passed in many wealthier nations have reduced smog in their cities, but problems from ground-level ozone and particulate matter continue to exist. In the United Kingdom, particulate matter is estimated to cause 10,000 deaths per year. In the United States, it is believed it could be as many as 60,000.

Particulate matter is also partly responsible for millions of cases of breathing disorders, such as asthma, bronchitis, and pneumonia. The number of people suffering from asthma is rising; in the USA alone, over 6 million children are asthma sufferers. Elsewhere in the world, especially in rapidly developing nations in Asia and Africa, the problems of air pollution are even more severe. China is home to half of the ten cities suffering the worst air pollution in the world.

Mexico City

One of the world's most polluted cities, Mexico City is set in a basin almost completely surrounded by hills and mountains. These help trap air pollution in the basin which reacts chemically with strong sunlight to form ground-level ozone. The basin is home to an estimated 20 million people and more than 4 million motor vehicles. Levels of key pollutants like ozone and nitrogen dioxide are many times the maximum safe limits. According to the World Health Organization, some 6,400 people die every year and more than 1 million suffer from permanent breathing problems due to air pollution there.

The ozone layer

At ground level, ozone is a dangerous pollutant, but when it is high in the atmosphere it shields the Earth's surface from the Sun's harmful **ultraviolet** rays. These rays can damage plant and ocean life, and cause skin cancers and other serious health problems. In 1985, British scientists discovered a "hole" (a very thinned area) in the ozone layer above Antarctica, approximately the size of the USA. In addition, the entire global ozone layer was found to have thinned slightly.

The chief cause was found to be the emission into the atmosphere of **CFCs**, chemicals which have only been produced since the 1930s. Chlorine is produced by the reaction of CFCs with ultraviolet rays from the Sun. One **atom** of chlorine can help to destroy 100,000 ozone molecules. CFCs break up slowly and scientists estimate that even if no more were sent into the atmosphere, it would take many years for the ozone layer to recover.

Acid rain

Pollution can be transfered to the sea or land and across country's borders. One example of this is acid rain. Sulphur dioxide and nitrogen oxides, particularly from coal-burning industries, can mix with water vapour in the air. These pollutants then fall as acid rain. Acid rain **erodes** stone, kills trees, and destroys life in rivers and, especially, lakes. Winds and air currents can cause acid rain to fall large distances from where the pollutants were generated.

This computer-generated image is a satellite map of the Antarctic region. The hole in the ozone layer is clearly shown as a dark blue area in the centre.

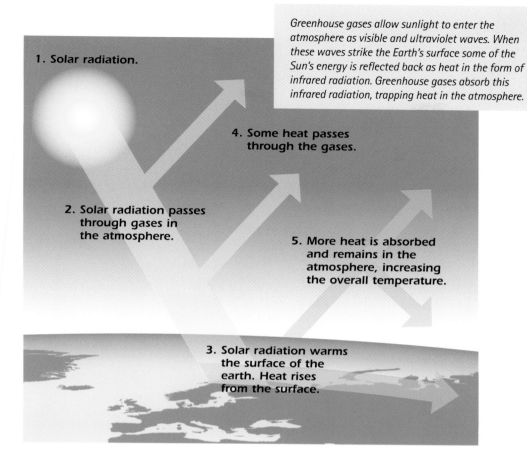

1. Solar radiation.

Greenhouse gases allow sunlight to enter the atmosphere as visible and ultraviolet waves. When these waves strike the Earth's surface some of the Sun's energy is reflected back as heat in the form of infrared radiation. Greenhouse gases absorb this infrared radiation, trapping heat in the atmosphere.

4. Some heat passes through the gases.

2. Solar radiation passes through gases in the atmosphere.

5. More heat is absorbed and remains in the atmosphere, increasing the overall temperature.

3. Solar radiation warms the surface of the earth. Heat rises from the surface.

Industrial pollution generated in the Great Lakes region of the USA is carried by north-easterly winds into Canada. There, acid rain has damaged or killed millions of trees and polluted some 14,000 lakes. Acid rain is declining in Europe and North America as a result of initiatives to reduce sulphur dioxide emissions. But elsewhere in the world, particularly in Asia, emissions are rising. In 2002, sulphur dioxide emissions in China from coal-burning power plants reached 6.6 million tonnes (a tenth of the world total). Large areas of China are now affected by acid rain, and in the Sichuan Basin region acid rain has destroyed 2,800 square kilometres (1,081 square miles) of forest, an area almost twice the size of Greater London.

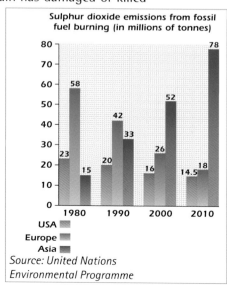

Sulphur dioxide emissions from fossil fuel burning (in millions of tonnes)

USA
Europe
Asia

Source: United Nations Environmental Programme

Global warming

The Earth is warming up. The ten hottest years on record have all occurred since 1990.

Most scientists believe that a major cause of this global warming is air pollution caused by human activity. Certain greenhouse gases occur naturally in the atmosphere and perform a crucial role in warming the Earth's surface. However, additional emissions of greenhouse gases from human activity run into millions of tonnes over the past 100 years. For example, human activity is pumping approximately 22,500 million tonnes of carbon dioxide into the atmosphere every year. These additional greenhouse gases are believed to be the principal causes of global warming.

Nitrous oxide 4%
Other pollutants 2%
CFCs 12%
Methane 20%
Carbon dioxide 62%

Gases which contribute to global warming
Source: Atmospheric Research and Information Centre

What is deforestation?

Deforestation also plays a major part in global warming. Often described as the "lungs of the planet", forests take in carbon dioxide from the air and generate much of the oxygen in the Earth's atmosphere. Deforestation is the removal of forests, either cut down for their wood, to be used as a material or fuel, or cleared to create more land for farming or new settlements. In the past 40 years, 45 per cent of the world's forests have disappeared. This has played a major part in reducing the Earth's ability to convert carbon dioxide into oxygen.

Top emitters of carbon dioxide from fossil fuels 1900-1999

	Total emissions (millions of tonnes)	Percentage of world total
USA	77,320	30.3%
Russia	22,721	8.9%
Germany	18,644	7.3%
China	17,786	7.0%
United Kingdom	14,336	5.6%
Japan	9,360	3.7%
France	7,241	2.8%
Ukraine	5,981	2.3%
Canada	5,831	2.3%
Poland	5,198	2.0%
India	5,098	2.0%
Italy	4,189	1.6%
South Africa	3,153	1.2%
Australia	2,736	1.1%
Czech Republic	2,565	1.0%

Source: World Resources Institute

What effects will global warming bring?

Global warming is a complex process and no one is exactly certain what will occur in the future. A rise in global temperature of just 2 or 3 °C (or 4–5 °F) could have a major impact on the planet. **Climate** change would lead to farmlands suffering, large areas of land becoming desert, and many species of plants and animals either migrating (moving) from the region or dying out. Many scientists believe that global warming could increase the speed at which the water cycle occurs. This would potentially create more violent weather phenomena, such as storms, hurricanes, floods, and droughts.

As global temperatures increase, sea levels will rise. The planet's ice caps will melt, the warmer water will expand and occupy more room than cooler water. Sea levels rose an estimated 20–30 centimetres (8–12 inches) in the 20th century, and many experts predict a further 40–80 centimetres (16–31 inches) rise throughout the 21st century. This rise would put at risk some of the world's largest food-growing areas which lie near the coast or around river deltas. Much of the food grown in China, Egypt, Bangladesh, and Vietnam, for example, is on land less than 3 metres (10 feet) above sea level.

Tuvalu under threat

Just a one-metre rise in sea level would submerge most of the land of the island nations of the Maldives, Marshall Islands, and Tuvalu, amongst others. Tuvalu consists of nine small islands in the Pacific Ocean, near Fiji, which are all less than 3 metres (10 feet) above sea level. Rising sea levels are claiming valuable land and contaminating freshwater drinking wells with seawater. Tuvalu's 11,000 islanders face an uncertain future.

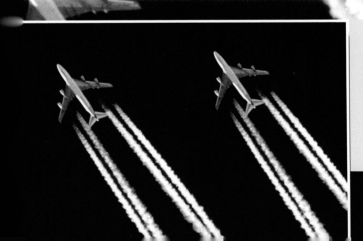

Air travel has boomed and today contributes around 600 million tonnes of carbon dioxide into the atmosphere each year, more than the entire UK output. There are also concerns that it will rise as the number of international air travellers is projected to double by 2018.

Water pollution

Water is fundamental to life on Earth. It covers almost three quarters of the planet's surface, but most is seawater. Only 0.07 per cent is available for use by people. This is the freshwater in lakes, rivers, and underground sources known as **aquifers**.

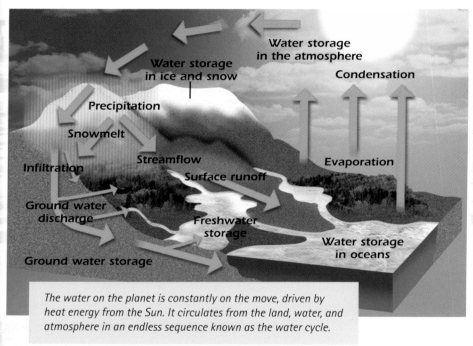

Water storage in the atmosphere

Water storage in ice and snow

Condensation

Precipitation

Snowmelt

Streamflow

Surface runoff

Evaporation

Infiltration

Ground water discharge

Freshwater storage

Water storage in oceans

Ground water storage

The water on the planet is constantly on the move, driven by heat energy from the Sun. It circulates from the land, water, and atmosphere in an endless sequence known as the water cycle.

Point source and non-point source pollution

Water pollution sources are often divided into two types. "Point source" is where pollutants reach water through a specific entry point, such as an oil tanker spillage or a drainpipe discharging sewage. "Non-point source" (NPS) pollution comes from different sources and can be harder to control. A common example of NPS pollution is "runoff". This is where rain or melting snow washes over land, picking up pollutants along the way, and eventually carries them into lakes and rivers. Oil, grease, and salt from roads, animal and human waste, and chemicals from industry and agriculture can all be NPS pollutants.

Industrial pollution

Industry generates pollution in a variety of ways. Some of these, such as buried waste on land and certain forms of air pollution (for example, acid rain) can be transformed into water pollution. Factories are often built beside rivers so that water can be used in their work. Sometimes they pump poisonous chemical waste into the water. Heat can also be a water pollutant. Power stations and other factories are often sited by a river or sea to use large amounts of water as a coolant. In some situations, returning this water, now much warmer, to the natural water source can damage the **ecosystem**.

Dumping

Rivers, lakes, and seas have been used as dumping grounds for unwanted objects and substances for centuries. The problem became far more serious during the 20th century with the massive increase in waste and consumer goods and the rise of the chemical and nuclear power industries. Between 1949 and 1983, a site some 800 kilometres (500 miles) southwest of Land's End in Britain was used by the UK, the Netherlands, Switzerland, and Belgium as a dumping ground for an estimated 100,000 tonnes of radioactive waste in barrels. Some of these containers have leaked and may have a long-term impact on marine life.

The world's most polluted water

Radioactive waste from nuclear power plants can also generate water pollution. Lake Karachai sits in western Siberia, Russia. Radioactive waste from the nearby Mayak nuclear power plant was pumped into the lake for almost 20 years. It is believed that the lake contains more **radioactivity** than was released by the entire Chernobyl nuclear accident. Lake Karachai lies within the Chelyabinsk region, which has one of the highest cancer rates in Russia.

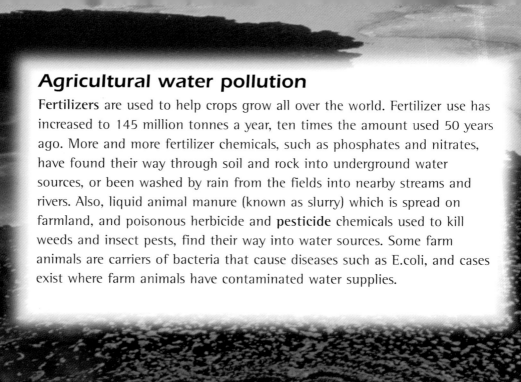

Agricultural water pollution

Fertilizers are used to help crops grow all over the world. Fertilizer use has increased to 145 million tonnes a year, ten times the amount used 50 years ago. More and more fertilizer chemicals, such as phosphates and nitrates, have found their way through soil and rock into underground water sources, or been washed by rain from the fields into nearby streams and rivers. Also, liquid animal manure (known as slurry) which is spread on farmland, and poisonous herbicide and **pesticide** chemicals used to kill weeds and insect pests, find their way into water sources. Some farm animals are carriers of bacteria that cause diseases such as E.coli, and cases exist where farm animals have contaminated water supplies.

An engineer inspects the pollution pouring from a pipeline into this lake.

24

Impacts on life

Water pollution can have a number of effects. Both animals and humans can be poisoned by water containing radioactive pollutants, toxic industrial chemicals, and waste **heavy metals,** such as arsenic, mercury, and lead. Sewage and other pollutants in water can help transmit disease. Pollutants in water are sometimes absorbed by plants or consumed by creatures and enter food chains. For example, the heavy metal, cadmium, found in some fertilizers, can be absorbed by crops, which if eaten in large enough amounts can cause diarrhoea-based illnesses and liver and kidney damage.

Many forms of water pollution can result in oxygen being used up or removed from water. For example, excess nitrogen can feed quick-growing **algae** which helps take oxygen from the water and can block out sunlight. This can kill off life in lakes and areas of sea. Over 140 "dead zones" – where there is not enough oxygen for life to exist – are found in seas throughout the world, many off the eastern coast of the USA and in the seas in and around Europe.

Farmers who spray fertilizers on their crops need to wear protective masks.

The Gulf of Mexico dead zone

The Mississippi river system is America's largest and drains 41 per cent of mainland USA. Its waters carry up to 1.6 million tonnes of nitrogen into the Gulf of Mexico every year. Half of this comes from fertilizers used on farmland which has run-off into streams and rivers which feed the Mississippi. The remainder comes from animal waste and industrial and sewage treatment waste water pumped into the Mississippi. This nitrogen has helped generate a gigantic dead zone in the Gulf of Mexico where little marine life exists. The dead zone is approximately 21,000km^2 (13,000 mi^2) in size, larger than Wales.

Oil and water

Oil can spill and spread over a large area of water, poisoning and killing plants and animals. According to the Oil Spill Intelligence Report, since 1960 there have been 49 spills of 34 tonnes of oil or more in the English Channel and 267 spills in the Gulf of Mexico. In August 2003, the *Tasmin Spirit* oil tanker spilled an estimated 15,000 tonnes along the coast of Pakistan. The oil devastated fishing grounds and put 90,000 Pakistani fishermen out of work.

Although spills from damaged oil tankers like the *Amoco Cadiz* and the *Exxon Valdez* reach the headlines, they only make up a fraction of the oil which pollutes water. Air pollution, mainly from cars and industry, puts hundreds of tonnes of pollutants from oil products into the oceans each year as rain washes these products out of the air and into oceans. The cleaning out of ship engines and tanker containers contributes to the oil pollution of oceans. Millions more litres of used oil from motor vehicles and machinery find their way into waterways and oceans. More than half of all Americans, for example, change their own oil, but only about one-third of this used oil is collected and recycled.

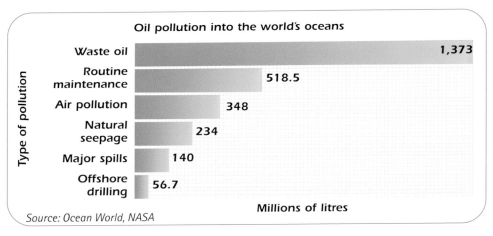

Oil pollution into the world's oceans

Type of pollution	Millions of litres
Waste oil	1,373
Routine maintenance	518.5
Air pollution	348
Natural seepage	234
Major spills	140
Offshore drilling	56.7

Source: Ocean World, NASA

Access to water

We take clean water for granted, but millions of people are affected by dry climates and droughts, which mean a lack of water in their region. Many millions more live near freshwater sources but ones which have been seriously polluted and are not safe to drink, wash, or cook with. The **United Nations (UN)** estimates that over 1.1 billion people lack access to a regular, clean, and safe water supply. The vast majority of these people live in the world's poorest nations.

Water, poverty, and disease

- The average person in the UK uses 334 litres (88 gallons) of water per day.
- The average person in the developing world uses 10 litres (2.6 gallons) per day.
- 40,000,000,000 hours are spent every year carrying water by people (mainly women) in Africa.
- Every 8 seconds, a child dies from a water-related disease.
- 50 per cent of people in developing countries suffer from a water-related disease.

Source: United Nations

This water standpipe, provided by the charity WaterAid, offers clean water to people who previously had to rely on polluted river sources. In 2002-2003, WaterAid helped over 640,000 people gain access to clean water supplies.

The problem of sewage

Vast amounts of sewage containing waste water from households and human waste is pumped into rivers, lakes, and seas. In wealthier, more developed countries, much of this is treated to remove some of the key pollutants. But half the world's population live in areas without adequate sewage systems and where sewage tends to be flushed straight back into streams and rivers without being treated. For example, Bangkok, the capital city of Thailand, discharges an estimated 10,000 tonnes of raw sewage and other waste into its rivers and canals every day.

In many developed countries, limits have been imposed on water pollution and once dirty rivers have been successfully cleaned up.

Many deadly diseases are carried or caused by this polluted water, either through eating food contaminated with this water, or via organisms such as bacteria which breed in the water. Water-related diseases, such as **cholera,** diarrhoea, and trachoma (which causes blindness or major health problems in six million people) is responsible for the deaths of more than 5.2 million people every year.

Access to safe water and life expectancy in selected countries, 2002

Country	Percentage of population without access to clean water	Life expectancy at birth (in years)
Afghanistan	87	43
Ethiopia	76	42
Chad	73	48
Sierra Leone	72	39
Angola	62	47
Papua New Guinea	58	42
Uganda	50	42
Vietnam	44	69
China	25	70
USA	0	77
UK	0	77

Source: World Bank, 2002

Cleaning up the world's water

Although it can take large sums of money and a long time, water pollution can be reduced and its effects reversed. Large "remediation" (clean-up) operations can help improve water quality, but new laws, agreements, and systems are essential to stop further pollution from occurring.

There have been successes. Phosphate levels in two of the Great Lakes of North America, Lake Ontario and Lake Erie, have dropped by over 75 per cent since the 1970s. In the UK, the River Thames was so polluted that in 1949 water samples from the river contained no oxygen. Yet, following major clean-up initiatives and stricter laws, the water quality has improved so much that in 2000, over 90 species of fish were found in its waters. But much more needs to be done to enable far more of the world's water to be clean and safe for all life.

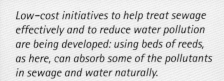

Low-cost initiatives to help treat sewage effectively and to reduce water pollution are being developed: using beds of reeds, as here, can absorb some of the pollutants in sewage and water naturally.

Land pollution

Land pollution is the degrading of the Earth's land. It can occur on different scales and cause harm in many ways. Litter, such as old wire or fishing line, can strangle birds and land animals. Large-scale burying or dumping of toxic chemicals on land can pollute and harm life over a large area.

Pollution on land is often then transferred into water. Seeping water through a rubbish or toxic waste dump can carry some of the harmful pollutants from the land into water sources.

Rubbish dumps

Most wealthier, developed countries generate millions of tonnes of solid waste or rubbish. In the USA, for example, an estimated 720 kilograms (1,587 pounds) of waste is generated per year for every person who lives there. Every family in the UK generates approximately a tonne of household rubbish per year.

This waste is disposed of in a number of ways, such as being burned in **incinerators**. Around half of all of the USA's household waste and over 80 per cent of UK waste is buried in dumps in the ground, called landfill sites. When full, most landfill sites in wealthier countries are landscaped and all looks well on the surface.

But environmentalists are concerned about what may be going on underneath. As the buried rubbish **decomposes**, it can form poisonous substances. Rainwater seeps through a landfill site and can produce a poisonous liquid called "leachate" which may enter underground water supplies, or even streams and rivers.

The decomposing rubbish can also generate large amounts of methane gas which, if not managed, can cause explosions. **Sanitary** landfill sites have been developed which provide a solid plastic or concrete barrier between the waste materials and the soil, but some environmentalists still fear that these barriers could be damaged and release pollutants into the soil and **groundwater.**

Love Canal

Throughout the 20th century, Love Canal in the US state of New York was an abandoned canal that was used as a dumping ground for around 22,000 tonnes of poisonous chemicals from industry. The canal was filled in with soil and around 100 houses and a school were built on the land. By the late 1970s, several hazardous chemicals had leaked through their metal containers or had risen to the surface. Investigations confirmed that poisonous substances were in the soil and that the area had high rates of birth defects, cancer, and other illnesses. Families were evacuated in 1978 and the site declared a national emergency. In the mid-1990s, the chemical company who owned the land agreed to pay national and state governments a total of US$227 million in compensation.

Pesticide pollution

As the world's population has boomed, the demand on farmland to produce more food has increased massively. Most farmers have turned to using chemical **pesticides** to kill insects which can harm or reduce the yield of a crop. Many of these pesticide chemicals can build to levels that harm the soil's ability to support crops and other life. They can also pollute water supplies. In the early 1990s, the United Nations estimated that some five million people a year suffer from serious pesticide poisoning. Persistent Organic Pollutants (POPs) are chemical substances that stay in the environment over a long period of time. There is great concern about POPs as they enter the food chain and build up in the fatty tissues of animals. Many POPs are pesticides.

Tackling land pollution

Land pollution can be combated in a number of ways. Some chemical pesticides and herbicides have been outlawed in many countries, although the polluting effects from their use in the past will take many years to disappear. Farming using natural, non-chemical forms of pest and weed control is an important way to lower chemical levels in the soil. Major community **recycling** schemes can also help reduce waste levels and save energy and resources.

Consumer demand for produce grown without pesticides has led to the expansion of organic farms in the developing world. Organic tea (left) is now widely available.

Individuals can make a difference in a number of ways. They can greatly cut back the amount of waste they generate by following the "three Rs":
- Reducing consumption (by buying longer-lasting items and items with less or no packaging)
- Reusing old items (by repairing damaged items and donating old items)
- Recycling waste like paper, plastic bottles, glass, and aluminium drinks cans.

Biodegradable

Many materials are biodegradable. This means they can rot and break down relatively quickly and safely by natural means, and be absorbed into the environment. Cotton rags, for example, can take between one and five months to break down. Other materials do not break down as quickly. Plastic bags can take 10-20 years, tin cans 50-100 years, and glass bottles a million years.

UK household waste (kilograms per person a year)			
	1983–1984	1991–1992	2002–2003
Total waste	397	428	521
Waste recycled	3	11	76

Source: UK Department of the Environment

Most plastics take a long time to break down and are a serious threat to wildlife. Every year, up to 2 million seabirds die as a result of eating, or get tangled up in, rubbish.

The debate over solutions

Pollution is causing harm all over the world. What is being done to tackle it? Many different initiatives are being introduced or worked on throughout the world. Some are based on technological breakthroughs, others as a result of national laws or international agreements between countries. Many more are the work of communities of ordinary people seeking to combat pollution in their local area.

Cleaner energy sources

Most of the world's electricity is generated by burning fossil fuels which release harmful pollutants into the atmosphere. Things can be improved, though. Devices called scrubbers remove as much as 95 per cent of sulphur dioxide and nitrogen dioxide emissions from electricity-generating power plants. The USA and Canada, for example, reduced their sulphur dioxide emissions by 28 per cent between 1980 and 1995 and, by 2010, aim to have halved emissions from 1980 levels.

Some countries have switched from power stations which burn coal to less polluting stations which burn **natural gas**. However, even natural gas power stations send large amounts of pollutants into the air.

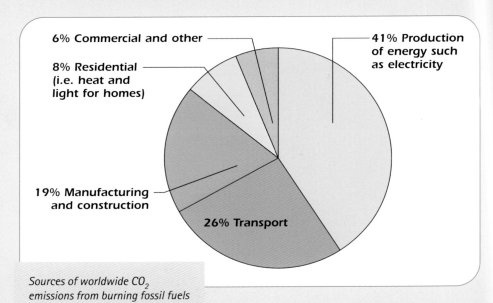

6% Commercial and other

8% Residential (i.e. heat and light for homes)

41% Production of energy such as electricity

19% Manufacturing and construction

26% Transport

Sources of worldwide CO$_2$ emissions from burning fossil fuels

ALTERNATIVE ENERGY

Alternative energy sources exist which are not only renewable, but also generate little or no pollution. Save for some noise pollution and the pollution generated in building them, wind turbines emit no dangerous substances as their blades turn to produce electricity. The same is true for solar panels and thermal water heaters, both of which use energy from the Sun. Critics of renewable energies maintain that they cannot supply the vast amounts of energy demanded by growing populations. But those in favour point out that they can make a major contribution to providing energy whilst reducing pollution greatly.

NUCLEAR POWER

Nuclear power is one of the least polluting of all major energy sources. It sends no emissions into the atmosphere and uses only small amounts of fuel to generate large amounts of electricity. Some countries with great increases in energy demand, such as India, are building new nuclear power stations. But public fears over the catastrophic damage that a major accident at a nuclear power plant could bring have seen development of nuclear power halted and power stations closed down in many countries.

This bus is one of a new generation of "cleaner" vehicles, powered by a hydrogen fuel cell.

Cleaner travel and transport

The fossil fuels burned by cars, lorries, and planes are a major source of air pollution, whilst discarded motor vehicles, fuels, and products such as car batteries pollute water and land. Yet, just like the demand for electricity, the numbers of motor vehicles in the world are expected to rise dramatically. In India's capital city, New Delhi, transport accounts for 65 per cent of all air pollution. In the last 25 years, the population has increased three times, but motor vehicle numbers have increased nearly 13 times.

Some countries have passed stricter laws on emissions from cars. They encourage car sharing and are striving to improve public transport which is more energy efficient and generates less pollution per passenger per trip.

Fuel efficiency of different types of vehicles can be measured in terms of how far a litre of fuel can carry a passenger.

One litre of fuel carries a passenger:
- 6.4 kilometres (4 miles) in a large car
- 8.8 kilometres (5.5 miles) in a small car
- 49 kilometres (30.5 miles) in a 40-seater bus

Technology has provided improvements such as lead-free petrol and cars which are more fuel-efficient. The brightest prospect is for vehicles powered by non-fossil fuels, such as hydrogen, which generates zero air pollution.

A hazy smog caused by atmospheric pollution is clearly visible over the city of Cairo in Egypt.

International laws and agreements

Whilst some pollution problems are found inside national borders, the most severe pollution issues the world faces are international. Agreements between nations to reduce pollution have had some success. For example, MARPOL is a UN treaty which became effective from 1983. It helped to reduce oil pollution at sea by almost 60 per cent during the 1980s and early 1990s. The **Montreal Protocol**, established in 1987, was designed to reduce the emissions of CFCs which threatened the ozone layer. World CFC production fell by 91 per cent between 1986 and 2002. The ozone layer is still being depleted as a result of CFCs in the past, but scientists estimate that the depletion has already slowed down by more than half.

The Kyoto Protocol

To some critics, international agreements are a good idea but mean nothing unless they are enforced fully and by all countries. The Kyoto Protocol of 1997 gave every industrial country a target to control and reduce its **greenhouse gas** emissions. The overall aim was to reduce global greenhouse gas emissions by 5.2 per cent by 2012. A number of nations are on target to reach their goal, but the agreement has had many difficulties. Some critics have argued that a 5 per cent cut is simply not enough to make a difference, and not all nations who initially signed the agreement are enforcing their reductions. The USA, responsible for a quarter of the total world CO_2 emissions, has not agreed to the protocol.

UNITED TO FIGHT CLIMATE CHANGE
KYOTO PROTOCOL 16-2-2005

In 2005, the Kyoto Protocol, that had been agreed in 1997, came into force. At the conference held to commemorate this achievement there was still much discussion about what countries could be doing to reduce emissions still further.

Short term v. long term

Scientists believe that many of the effects of pollution on the environment can be halted or reversed. But they also believe that it will take a massive effort. With many pollutants having a long life – CFCs, for example, can last over 100 years in the atmosphere – it will also take a long time.

Most people think only about the present and the next couple of years ahead. Many governments are elected to power for short periods of 4 or 5 years. Whilst the majority of people believe a less polluted, cleaner environment is a good thing, they are reluctant to reduce their high standard of living, or pay higher taxes or prices for goods and energy produced. Industries also put pressure on governments, arguing that slashing pollution would greatly increase costs and force them to put people out of work and raise prices.

Cleaning up Lake Taihu

A five-year programme is underway to clean up the third largest freshwater lake in China, Lake Taihu. The lake, a major source of drinking water for some 40 million people, has been heavily polluted by untreated sewage, pesticides, fertilizers, and industrial waste. There are 243 different projects, including 81 sewage disposal plants, being built at a cost of US$2,600,000,000. This figure is likely to increase as pollution levels in the lake are still rising. A major part of the problem is that local industries are ignoring the new laws and still pump polluting waste into the lake.

Costs of pollution

Some people want to see strict pollution guidelines imposed on every nation, but many poorer, developing nations argue that this is unfair. The poorest nations consume a fraction of the goods, services, and energy of the wealthiest nations. Many poorer countries are developing their industries to try to provide their people with a higher standard of living and this, in turn, is generating increasing levels of pollution. Do people in these nations have the right to electricity just like the majority of the world's population, even if that were to create more pollution?

Clearing up and reducing future pollution costs large sums of money. Many poorer countries, struggling to provide the most basic of services to their people, argue that they simply cannot afford to use the least polluting energy and manufacturing techniques. Many of these nations also point out that it is the wealthier countries that have generated most of the world's pollution. Just 15 countries, including the USA, the UK, Germany, Japan, and France, generate 79 per cent of all CO_2 emissions. Many less developed nations question why they should be forced to agree to decisions made by more developed countries who have been both the biggest polluters in the past, and remain so today.

Improving the terrible living conditions endured by many of their people may be more of a priority for governments in developing countries, than enforcing international decisions on pollution control.

A clean future?

Many of the things people do which cause pollution are likely to increase in the near future. The world's population is rising and may top 8 billion by 2030. Two thirds of the world's people are expected to live in cities by that time. More countries are seeking to develop their industries. Motor vehicle numbers are increasing and, if they increase at the present rate, will reach more than 1 billion by 2025. Many predictions for the future are gloomy. Global warming is expected to have a major impact on the planet later in the 21st century. The World Health Organization estimates that by 2025 as many as 8 million people per year could die due to pollution-related health problems, unless massive attempts are made to curb the rising tide of air, water, and land pollution.

Many environmental groups organize activities that young people can get involved in. Here, volunteers collect rubbish from a beach.

Advances in energy-efficient technology and growing use of non-polluting **renewable energy** sources and vehicle fuels would help. Stricter international agreements and tough laws in individual countries will probably be necessary. But these will only work if they are backed by large sums of money to fund alternative ways of producing goods and services. Finally, individuals must make small but crucial changes in the way that they live. As shown by the large drop in sulphur dioxide emissions in some countries, and the global lowering of CFCs, there have already been notable breakthroughs and successes. But much, much more has to be done if the world population is going to enjoy as clean and unpolluted a planet as their ancestors did in the past.

Ten things you can do to help reduce pollution

- Walk or cycle short journeys instead of taking a car ride. Encourage your family, neighbours, and friends to do the same.
- Make your home use less energy by switching off lights, installing energy efficient compact fluorescent light bulbs, and by setting heating and air conditioning levels to use less energy.
- Boil only the amount of water you need. Every cup boiled uses electricity that equals approximately 25 cups of released carbon dioxide.
- Many electrical items still consume electricity when plugged into the mains. Unplug all electrical items when not in use.
- Use phosphate-free detergents and cleaning products.
- Use rechargeable batteries rather than disposable ones.
- Start a local or community scheme to plant trees in your neighbourhood.
- Recycle paper, glass, aluminium, and other materials.
- Reuse as many objects and materials, such as carrier bags, as possible. This saves both energy and waste, both of which can cause pollution.
- Investigate where pollution prevention and clean-up schemes exist in your area and join in.

Statistical information

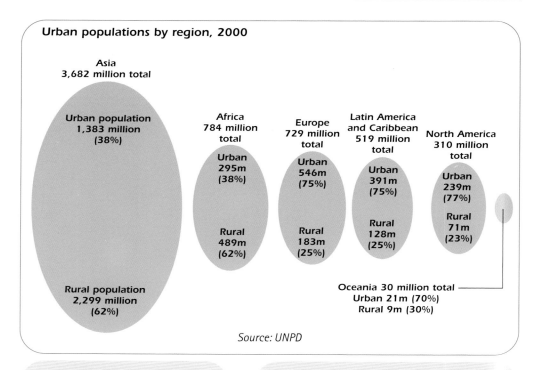

Urban populations by region, 2000

Asia
3,682 million total

Urban population
1,383 million
(38%)

Rural population
2,299 million
(62%)

Africa
784 million total

Urban
295m
(38%)

Rural
489m
(62%)

Europe
729 million total

Urban
546m
(75%)

Rural
183m
(25%)

Latin America
and Caribbean
519 million total

Urban
391m
(75%)

Rural
128m
(25%)

North America
310 million total

Urban
239m
(77%)

Rural
71m
(23%)

Oceania 30 million total
Urban 21m (70%)
Rural 9m (30%)

Source: UNPD

Countries with greatest increase in motor vehicles 1980–1998

South Korea	1,514%
Thailand	692%
Nigeria	550%
China	300%
Pakistan	300%
Uganda	300%
Turkey	252%
India	250%
Poland	217%
Indonesia	175%

Source: World Bank

Top ten nitrogen oxide polluting countries

	Kilograms of nitrogen oxide per person
Australia	118
Iceland	106
USA	80
Canada	68
Finland	51
Norway	51
Denmark	47
New Zealand	46
Czech Republic	41
Luxembourg	40

Source: Organization for Economic Cooperation and Development

Air pollution in selected world cities

City	Population (millions)	Suspended particles levels (mg/m³) 90*	Sulphur dioxide levels (mg/m³) 50*	Nitrogen dioxide levels (mg/m³) 50*
Amsterdam	1.1	40	10	58
Athens	3.1	178	34	64
Beijing	11.3	377	90	122
Berlin	3.3	50	18	26
Brussels	1.1	78	20	48
Bombay	15.1	240	33	39
Cairo	9.9	–	69	–
Copenhagen	1.3	61	7	54
Dublin	0.9	–	20	–
Havana	2.2	–	1	5
Kuala Lumpur	1.2	85	24	–
London	7.6	–	25	77
Los Angeles	12.4	–	9	74
Mexico City	16.6	279	74	130
Milan	4.3	77	31	248
Montreal	3.3	34	10	42
Moscow	9.3	100	109	–
New York	16.3	–	26	79
Singapore	2.8	–	20	30
Sydney	3.6	54	28	–
Tokyo	27.0	49	18	68

Source: World Bank
* World Health Organization Recommended Maximum levels

Glossary

acid rain rain, snow, and fog containing poisonous or harmful acidic chemicals, created by burning fossil fuels

algae primitive plants, including seaweeds and pond scum

altitude height, usually above sea level, of a particular point

aquifer underground water supply, often tapped for domestic use

atmosphere collection of gases that surround Earth

atom smallest unit of matter that can take part in a chemical reaction

chlorofluorocarbons (CFCs) series of man-made chemicals used in fridges, aerosols, and solvents

cholera infectious disease of the small intestine that is carried by bacteria

climate general weather conditions of a region or the entire Earth over a long period of time

decompose become rotten

ecosystem collection of all living things and their non-living surroundings in a defined area

emission harmful gas released into the air by industry, fires, and motor vehicles

enhanced greenhouse effect build-up of carbon dioxide, methane, and other gases in the atmosphere, trapping the Sun's heat and affecting the climate

environment physical surroundings

epidemic rapid spread of disease

erode to wear away

fertilizer substance which enriches soil and enables it to support more plant growth

food chain links between different animals that feed on plants and other animals

fossil fuel material which has been formed from decayed living things, and can be burned to generate energy

global warming warming-up of the Earth's surface due to changes in the gases within the Earth's atmosphere

greenhouse gas gas in the atmosphere that traps heat from the Sun and warms the Earth

groundwater water beneath the earth's surface that supplies the water tapped by wells, or that flows from springs

heavy metals metallic elements, such as cadmium, lead, and mercury, which can be poisonous

herbicide substance used as a weed killer when growing crops

incinerator device used to burn solid waste

industrialization process in which more emphasis is placed upon industry and manufacturing in a country's economy

ingest take a substance into the body, usually by eating or drinking
insecticide substance used to kill insects

methane natural gas
Montreal Protocol international agreement setting out targets and timetables for phasing out the use of CFCs

natural gas mixture of methane and other gases found underground or below the seabed, which can be used as a fuel

ozone layer thin layer of the atmosphere consisting of ozone gas. It absorbs most of the harmful ultraviolet rays from the Sun

pesticide poisonous substance which kills animal or insect pests
PM10 microscopic particles in the atmosphere such as dust, dirt, smoke and soot
precipitation water that falls from the atmosphere, such as rain, snow, or hail

radioactivity harmful rays and particles given off by certain substances as their atoms split apart
recycling recovering waste material to make new products. Can also mean to re-use discarded products.
renewable energy energy from a source which can be restored and maintained, such as wind and solar energy

resources natural things found on Earth, which can be used such as metals, trees, coal, or water
respiration chemical process in which food is broken down to release energy

sanitary free from dirt or bacteria that can cause disease
sewage waste, usually including waste water and human sewage
smog haze caused by smoke or atmospheric pollution

toxic harmful or poisonous substance

ultraviolet invisible form of light from the Sun which causes sunburn and can cause blindness and cancer
United Nations (UN) international organization, founded in 1945, to promote peace, security, and economic development
urban to do with the city or town

World Health Organization (WHO) international body concerned with the health and wellbeing of the planet's population

Further reading

Books

Baines, John. *Keeping The Air Clean* (Wayland, 1997)
Written by an award-winning environmentalist, this book looks in detail at the technical issues surrounding the many causes and forms of air pollution and the potential solutions.

Chapman, Matthew and Bowden, Rob. *21st Century Debates: Air Pollution* (Hodder Wayland, 2003)
This book gives a detailed look at the issue of air pollution, its causes, and its impacts, with a number of case studies from around the world.

Collinson, Alan. *Pollution* (Evans Brothers, 1997.)
Part of a series studying natural and man-made disasters, this book traces the history of human impact on Earth and the pollution people have generated from ancient times until the end of the 20th century.

Cooper, Adrian, Bowden, Rob and Bingley, Richard. *Just The Facts: Global Pollution* (Heinemann, 2002)
This is a clear, simple guide to world pollution, filled with statistics.

Contact Addresses

Australian Conservation
Foundation (ACF)
Floor 1
60 Leicester Street
Carlton
Victoria 3053
Australia
Tel: 03 9345 1111

Canadian Centre for Pollution
Prevention (C2P2)
100 Charlotte Street
Sarnia
Ontario
N7T 4R2
Canada
Tel: (1 800) 667 9790

Earth Policy Institute
1350 Connecticut Avenue, NW
Suite 403
Washington DC 20036
USA
Tel: (202) 496-9290

Friends Of The Earth
26-28 Underwood Street
London
N1 7JQ
UK
Tel: 020 7490 1555

National Society for Clean Air and
Environmental Protection – NSCA
44 Grand Parade
Brighton
BN2 2QA
UK
Tel: 01273 878770

Worldwatch Institute
1776 Massachusetts Avenue, NW
Washington, DC 20036
USA
Tel 202 452 1999

Websites

Centre for Renewable Energy and Sustainable Technology
http://www.crest.org/
This website includes news and information on energy application in the
United States.

Greenpeace
http://www.greenpeace.org
The international organization which promotes environmental awareness
and understanding has comprehensive news and report sections on
climate change.

National Oceanic and Atmospheric Administration
http://response.restoration.noaa.gov/kids/kids.html
A dedicated younger reader's section of this website has a detailed
breakdown of the issue of oil pollution of water and land, and looks at
attempts at prevention and clean–up operations.

World Health Organization
http://www.who.int/topics/en/
A collection of topics which concern the World Health Organization (WHO),
including indoor air pollution, water quality, and waste management are
discussed on this site.

Index